TRACING CATHOLIC ANCESTORS

Public Record Office
Pocket Guides to Family History

Getting Started in Family History

Using Birth, Marriage and Death Records

Using Census Returns

Using Wills

Using Army Records

Using Navy Records

Tracing Irish Ancestors

Tracing Scottish Ancestors

Using Poor Law Records

Tracing Catholic Ancestors

Tracing Nonconformist Ancestors

TRACING

CATHOLIC ANCESTORS

Michael Gandy

PUBLIC RECORD OFFICE

Public Record Office
Richmond
Surrey
TW9 4DU

ISBN 1 903365 05 8

Front cover: Bishop Brindle,
Roman Catholic Bishop of Nottingham
Photograph by Ephraim Pope Short of Nottingham
Registered by him for copyright 21 March 1902
(COPY 1/454)

Printed by Cromwell Press, Trowbridge, Wiltshire

CONTENTS

INTRODUCTION

This Pocket Guide concentrates on the records that relate to Catholic family history in England. Most of the text also applies to Wales, but many of the records of Scotland are arranged differently and are therefore beyond the scope of this guide. It is not intended to explain how to research ancestry in Ireland (see the PRO Pocket Guide, *Tracing Irish Ancestors*), although there is a good deal of material about Irish people who came to England.

It is assumed that you know basically how English and Welsh family history records work, and therefore only the Catholic aspects of the main state and Church of England (Anglican) records are explained here. Almost all modern series of family history records contain references to Catholics but in contexts where their religion is not the point. For more information on these records, read other Pocket Guides in the series, particularly *Getting Started in Family History*, *Using Birth, Marriage and Death Records*, *Using Census Returns* and *Using Wills*.

Tracing your family history is a fascinating and very personal piece of detective work. Some records are very easy to access, and it is possible for your research to progress rapidly. Other records are less easy to access and interpret, demanding skills which take time and perseverance to acquire. Either way, the potential satisfactions are enormous.

Historical background

Until the Reformation everyone in England and Wales was Catholic, but since the 16th century Catholics have been a minority. From 1559 to 1778 it was illegal to attend Catholic services, and after 1581 it was 'death for a priest to breathe the air of England'. These years are known as the Penal Period and during this time Catholics were often known as papists or, more formally, as recusants (from the Latin 'they refuse').

Most of the anti-Catholic laws had been repealed by 1829, and since the 1840s Catholics have made up between 5 and 10 per cent of the population, depending on whether you count the people who called themselves Catholic but were not regular churchgoers.

In some parts of England, particularly Lancashire, Catholicism survived quite strongly in the 17th and 18th centuries. In others it died out almost entirely until the arrival of Irish migrants in the 1840s and later. Many immigrants from Catholic countries such as France, Spain and Italy brought their religion with them, and there were also large groups from the Black Forest area of Germany. Nowadays numbers are swelled particularly by new arrivals from Nigeria and the Philippines.

ARCHIVES AND OTHER SOURCES

Below we give addresses to contact in the course of your Catholic family history research. There are a range of archives, libraries and societies to help; however, it is important to remember that after 1837 most of the important records for tracing family history (including that of Catholics) were compiled by the state and can be found either in the Public Record Office or the Family Records Centre.

Public Record Office (PRO)

The Public Record Office is the national repository for government records in the UK. It holds a wealth of records available for research. There is also an extensive library, with a unique collection of books and periodicals on family history as well as other aspects of history.

▼ **Public Record Office**
Kew
Richmond
Surrey TW9 4DU
General telephone: 020 8876 3444
Telephone number for enquiries and advance document orders: 020 8392 5200
Internet: http://www.pro.gov.uk/

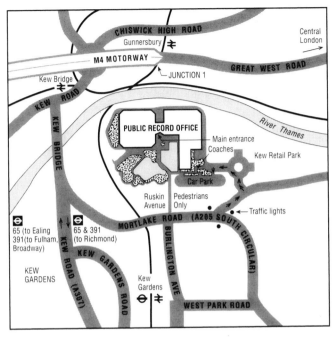

How to find the Public Record Office, Kew

Opening times (closed Sundays and Bank Holidays, and the Saturday of Bank Holiday weekends):

Monday	9 a.m. to 5 p.m.
Tuesday	10 a.m. to 7 p.m.
Wednesday	9 a.m. to 5 p.m.
Thursday	9 a.m. to 7 p.m.
Friday	9 a.m. to 5 p.m.
Saturday	9.30 a.m. to 5 p.m.

No appointment is needed to visit the PRO in Kew, but you will need a reader's ticket to gain access to the research areas. To obtain a ticket, take with you a full UK driving licence or a UK banker's card or a passport if you are a British citizen, and your passport or national identity card if you are not. Note that the last time for ordering documents is 4 p.m. on Mondays, Wednesdays and Fridays; 4.30 p.m. on Tuesdays and Thursdays; and 2.30 p.m. on Saturdays.

Family Records Centre (FRC)

The Family Records Centre is a service for family historians, set up in 1997 by the Office for National Statistics (ONS) and the Public Record Office. It gathers together a range of resources and research facilities specifically designed with family historians in mind. The major holdings include:

- indexes to births, marriages and deaths in England and Wales from 1 July 1837

- census returns 1841–1891

- death duty registers 1796–1858, indexes 1796–1902

- wills and administrations of the Prerogative Court of Canterbury 1383–1858

- many nonconformist registers 1567–1837

▶ **Family Records Centre**
1 Myddelton Street
London EC1R 1UW
General telephone: 020 8392 5300
Telephone for birth, marriage and death certificates:
0151 471 4800
Fax: 020 8392 5307
Internet: http://www.pro.gov.uk/
ONS website: http://www.ons.gov.uk/

Opening times (closed Sundays and Bank Holidays):

Monday	9 a.m. to 5 p.m.
Tuesday	10 a.m. to 7 p.m.
Wednesday	9 a.m. to 5 p.m.
Thursday	9 a.m. to 7 p.m.
Friday	9 a.m. to 5 p.m.
Saturday	9.30 a.m. to 5 p.m.

You can visit the FRC in person without an appointment at the opening times shown.

Society of Genealogists (SoG)

The Society of Genealogists is the best place to combine work on Catholic and non-Catholic secondary sources. The library contains a large collection of records and finding aids, some of which are unique. It covers Scottish and Irish records as well as English and Welsh, and has much on local history as well as genealogy. It has the largest collection of copies of parish registers in the UK and also an extensive collection of family histories and one-name studies.

▼ **Society of Genealogists (SoG)**
   14 Charterhouse Buildings
   Goswell Road
   London EC1M 7BA
   Telephone: 020 7251 8799
   Internet: http://www.sog.org.uk/

Opening times (closed Sundays and Mondays):

Tuesday	10 a.m. to 6 p.m.
Wednesday	10 a.m. to 8 p.m.
Thursday	10 a.m. to 8 p.m.
Friday	10 a.m. to 6 p.m.
Saturday	10 a.m. to 6 p.m.

You do not have to be a member of the Society of Genealogists to use its library, although you do have to pay a fee. You can visit it without an appointment. It is conveniently located for you to combine a trip there with a trip to the FRC.

Specialist societies and libraries

Before 1837, and especially before 1778, when Catholicism was illegal, tracing a Catholic family involves special records and specialized knowledge. Many people with a wider interest have collected and catalogued sources, compiled indexes and edited records for publication. There are quite a large number of specialist collections and societies. The following are the most important:

▼ Catholic Record Society (CRS)
Secretary:
12 Melbourne Place
Wolsingham
Durham DL13 3EH

Founded in 1904, the CRS has published 77 volumes in its well-known blue series. These include a great many baptism and marriage registers, records of the training colleges, schools and convents abroad, and transcripts of PRO records and important private papers. All volumes are either fully indexed or arranged alphabetically.

As well as the blue record series, CRS has published a number of occasional volumes, particularly the very important 'Return of Papists' of 1767. Since 1950 the CRS journal, *Recusant History*, has carried articles of importance on many aspects of Catholic local history which help us understand the background to our ancestors' lives.

▶ **Catholic Family History Society (CFHS)**
Secretary:
45 Gates Green Road
West Wickham
Kent BR4 9DE

Founded in 1983, CFHS works in parallel with the county family history societies to advise on the specialist aspects of Catholic family history in England, Scotland and Wales, and on the Irish communities in those countries. Its journal, *Catholic Ancestor*, also contains many valuable articles and transcripts of records.

▶ **Catholic Archives Society (CAS)**
Secretary:
Innyngs House
Hatfield Park
Hatfield
Herts AL9 5PL

The CAS was founded in 1980 to provide a forum for nearly a hundred archivists in charge of the Catholic records of dioceses and religious orders. The latter often have a great deal of material relating not only to their members but also to the missions, schools, hospitals, old people's homes and foreign missions with which they have been associated. Its journal, *Catholic Archives*, describes a great many collections, mostly in England but also in Ireland and elsewhere, and its directory lists the names and addresses of the archivists.

The books and work of CRS and CAS are vital, but it is not worth contacting them with a request for advice on a specific family history point. That is one of the purposes of CFHS.

Apart from the above there are a number of local societies, most of which publish a journal with useful articles. Enquire through your local library for copies of *Northern Catholic History, North West Catholic History, South West Catholic History, Gloucester and Avon Catholic History, Staffordshire Catholic History* and *Worcester Recusant* (the last two recently combined to publish *Midlands Catholic History*). *London Recusant, Essex Recusant* and *Kent Recusant* have all ceased to publish but produced good material in their time. Recently a very active group in South Wales started to publish *Yr Hen Ffydd (The Old Faith)*. Many of the diocesan newspapers carry historical articles and there are a very large number of individual parish histories.

For a full analysis of published material, read M. Gandy, *Catholic Family History: A Bibliography of General Sources* and *Catholic Family History: A Bibliography of Local Sources* (see Further Reading on p. 64).

The *Catholic Directory* is the most important source for up-to-date addresses, and old editions can be used to trace the whereabouts and history of orphanages and other institutions from years ago. It is arranged by diocese and lists every Catholic parish with the name and address of the parish priest. There are details of diocesan organizations, including the diocesan archives, local schools, societies and the religious orders working in the area. There are national sections for the religious orders, chaplaincies, Catholic societies and the caring services, such as the Catholic childrens' societies. The current *Catholic Directory* can be found in most larger public libraries and there is a full set at the Catholic Central Library, which holds the best collection of books on English Catholic history.

▼ **Catholic Central Library**
Lancing Street
London NW1 1ND
Telephone: 020 7383 4333
Email: librarian@catholic-library.demon.co.uk

The library is close to Euston Station, and open Monday to Friday without appointment.

Most diocesan archives (see below) have excellent collections, and there are a number of others in religious libraries and public schools that are open to the public by arrangement. A small number of second-hand book dealers specialize in English Catholic history, as well as other aspects of Catholicism.

Since 1850 England and Wales have been divided into Catholic dioceses. Most dioceses publish a diocesan directory which contains local information. Each diocese also has a diocesan archive and archivist. In many cases these archivists have put the records of most interest to family historians into the local record office (county record office).

Many of the older registers have been microfilmed or microfiched and some can be bought fairly cheaply. Some of the early registers are in the PRO and are included on the *International Genealogical Index (IGI)*, which can be consulted at the FRC, SoG and other record offices, and is now available on the internet at www.familysearch.org.

The addresses of diocesan archives can be found in the *Catholic Directory*. Details of local record offices can be found in J. Gibson and P. Peskett, *Record Offices: How to Find Them* (see p. 62) or by phoning the appropriate County or Town Hall.

A high proportion of the important material for research in the 16th, 17th and 18th centuries is in the Public Record Office, but some is in the Parliamentary Archives or in local record offices or Anglican diocesan record offices (which are often the same place).

▼ Parliamentary Archives
House of Lords
London SW1A 0PW
Telephone: 020 7219 3074
Fax: 020 7219 2570
Email: hlro@parliament.uk
Internet: http://www.parliament.uk/

Opening times are Monday to Friday 9.30 a.m. to 5 p.m.; Tuesday until 8 p.m. One week's notice is required. Readers should show confirmation of appointment and identification at the Pass Office.

Many important records belong to the private families that protected Catholics in many parts of England when the pressure was greatest. The Royal Commission on Historical Manuscripts has a database (searchable online) showing where many thousands of collections of private records are held.

▼ **Royal Commission on Historical Manuscripts**
   Quality House
   Quality Court
   Chancery Lane
   London WC2A 1HP
   Telephone: 020 7242 1198
   Fax: 020 7831 3550
   Email: nra@hmc.gov.uk
   Internet: http://www.hmc.gov.uk/

The rest of this guide is arranged in two parts. The first part explains the main sources for tracing Catholics since 1829. From the 1840s, when Irish immigrants arrived in England in large numbers, the majority of Catholics have been urban, working class and of Irish origin. The second part explains the sources for tracing the English recusants of the years 1559–1829, who mostly lived in the country areas of northern England. Many people today are descended from both groups and take pride in this ancestry.

It may seem odd to put the later section before the earlier section, but it is a basic rule of family history that we research backwards from today. In our work, the 19th century comes before the 18th!

PART ONE:
RESEARCH SINCE 1829

Family knowledge and documents

The first step in all family history research is for you and
your relatives to gather existing knowledge and clues.

You may start with a tradition of Catholicism: photographs of a first communion, mass or memorial cards,
newspaper cuttings about a wedding or funeral in a
Catholic church, or tales of old aunts who were nuns.
Family information may be written in a missal or prayer
book.

Other families have no tradition of Catholicism but find it
as they trace back. Religion is both a family attachment
and a personal choice. Some people convert either in or out,
while others may lapse from regular practice without feeling that they have lapsed for ever. Many people marry out
and it is not always obvious at the outset which religious
choices the new family will make. Children may have
attended a Catholic school or even been in an orphanage
without Catholicism being their religion or that of their
parents. Always approach your research with an open
mind.

Many Catholics have come from outside England. Other
relatives may have gone to Australia or America or
elsewhere, and the records of those countries may be as
useful as the ones here. This is particularly the case when

English records just say 'born Ireland' and more precise information is needed to continue the research.

Catholic records of Catholics

In Catholic countries the Catholic church has a parish system very much like the Anglican system in England, and priests keep registers that are equivalent to the Church of England parish registers. England, however, was defined as a missionary country until after the First World War and the rules were not the same.

In the 19th century Catholic parishes did not have defined boundaries and were usually known as missions. Like the nonconformists, their churches were often called chapels (especially the smaller churches).

Until the 18th century it was unsafe for priests to keep registers of the sacraments they administered; such registers, if confiscated, would have been their death warrant. The oldest Catholic register in England – that of Baddesley Clinton in Warwickshire – begins in 1657. Like many early registers, it was the notebook of a priest who did not have a safe base but travelled round the countryside. The registers that are now at Worcester begin in 1685, but the priest who compiled them did not arrive at Worcester until 1720. Many older missions developed from private chapels in gentry houses, and a large number of registers for missions of this type start between 1720 and 1760.

Most of the new industrial towns attracted Catholics from Ireland, and a large number of new missions were founded all through the 19th century. The congregations themselves were often too poor to help towards building a church, and the priests had no other resources. The enormous influx of the late 1840s (because of the famine in Ireland) swamped the already struggling missions. It took at least twenty years for provision to begin to catch up with need, and the developing situation can be seen year by year in the *Catholic Directory*.

Parish records

By the 1840s Catholicism had been legal in England for over 60 years and proper records were being kept. The more formal records are likely to be in Latin, but translation and interpretation are just a matter of practice.

The following are the three basic series of records that any Catholic parish is likely to have. Earlier records may be in the local record office, but many are still with the parish priest. A full analysis of the registers available for each parish, with their whereabouts and the existence of copies, has been published in M. Gandy, *Catholic Missions and Registers 1700–1880* (see p. 62).

- **Baptism registers** give the name of the child and its parents, the dates of baptism and birth, and the names of the godparents (also known as sponsors). The register does not usually record where the parents lived or their occupation, but it does give the mother's maiden name – an enormous plus.

Many later baptisms have annotations recording where the child married in later life. This follows a change in church rules in 1908 and is obviously very useful.

- **Confirmation registers** are more or less a census of the young children (probably aged around seven to nine in the 19th century). Name, surname and religious name are recorded but no other information. The religious name was a personal choice and usually had no family significance. In a high proportion of cases the boys took Patrick and the girls took Mary.

  When dioceses were established in 1850, some bishops began to keep a central list of all the children they had confirmed. Such registers exist up to the 1890s for most of the south of England. Much of this material should also be in the parish registers, but not all confirmations were in parishes and the bishops' books include the confirmations of adult converts and confirmations in schools and prisons.

- **Marriage registers** often give very little information, just the names of the couple, the date and the witnesses. In the years 1754 to 1837 all Catholics had to be married in the Anglican church; some had a Catholic ceremony as well, although many didn't. After 1837 Catholic registers may contain less information than required by the form for state registration, but some priests went one better and recorded the names of both parents, including the mother's maiden name, and/or place of birth and place of parents' residence. These registers, which are quite common, are obviously a great help in tracing a family back to Ireland.

In the 20th century couples intending to marry had to complete a form recording, among other things, place of baptism. Many parishes have these, but they are unlikely to go back before the 1920s, if so far.

In mixed marriages the non-Catholic partner sometimes had to sign a paper promising not to oppose the children being brought up Catholic. These papers sometimes survive if they were slipped into the register.

There are a number of other types of records which were kept in some parishes but not all. Many of these were working documents and there was no obligation to keep them, but a good deal of material may still survive uncatalogued in church cupboards:

- **Deaths**. Most Catholic churches had no burial ground, and priests knew that the burial would be properly recorded either by the Anglican minister or the cemetery authorities. Some priests kept death registers, however, and the printed form has a space to record where the body was buried. Apart from that, the only information usually given is the name and age of the deceased.

- **Obituaries**. Every parish has a list of the dead arranged by date so that they can be prayed for publicly on the anniversary of their death. There have always been formal or informal lists of those for whom Masses must be said.

- **Status animarum**. Sometimes priests drew up an account of the congregation. These might go into some detail about particular families, especially those who gave cause for concern. The accounts are likely to be more complete for the smaller congregations, and a number of them have been published with the old mission registers in various volumes of the CRS (see p. 15).

  For many years annual statistics of baptisms, marriages and converts have been sent in to the bishops, but they do not contain any names.

- **Parish census**. Many parishes have compiled these over the years. They are often annotated with alterations (not necessarily systematically).

- **Easter communions**. These lists show who was doing at least their minimal duty. They are usually found in small parishes, as it would have been difficult to keep tabs on everyone in a large parish.

- **Sick calls**. Some priests noted who they had visited, especially when they were called out to give the last rites. These books occasionally survive.

Guilds and fraternities

Many Catholics used their parish as a social centre as well as a religious one. Larger parishes often had organizations to suit all tastes. Some, such as the annual Walks, with sashes and banners and best clothes for the children, related to local events. Many were local branches of national organizations (with perhaps a national magazine in which they might be mentioned); some were in aid of the missions or the poor and others were purely social – dances, football clubs, scouts and guides. There were often collections and subscriptions, and plenty of news to put in the parish magazine. Despite wide circulation at the time, parish magazines do not often survive and should be kept carefully if they are found. However, many events found their way into local newspapers, both Catholic and non-Catholic.

Amongst the most important national organizations run through local branches were:

- **Bona Mors (The Confraternity of a Happy Death)**. The monthly Mass for deceased members was a good combination of an act of charity and a get-together. Lists may survive of living or deceased members. The Rosary Confraternities were based on the same idea.

- **Society of St Vincent de Paul (SVP)**. This offered practical help for the poor, tiding specific families over bad times. The minutes of each branch can be interesting and occasionally there are reports on each family that was visited, with details of Catholicity (including place of baptism and marriage), schools, work history, illnesses and income.

The SVP is still very active, as are the Catenians and the Knights of St Columba. The older records of these organizations, where they survive, will probably be held by the parish priest.

Converts

For ordinary people the only record of conversion will be the record of baptism. It will probably be marked as conditional, but *any* baptism of an adult is likely to be a conversion, as Catholic parents always had their children baptized as quickly as possible. Adults going for confirmation are almost certain to be converts.

Priests who received soldiers into the church in the First World War reported the fact to the Archdiocese of Westminster, and CFHS has a list of those involved. In 1908 the Archdiocese of Westminster began a central register of converts for that diocese (London, Middlesex, Hertfordshire and Essex). This is arranged by date and enables a searcher to find out in which church the convert was received, but does not give any indication of circumstances or motives. No similar registers for the other dioceses are known.

In the 19th century many converts of importance were trumpeted as signs that the whole of England would soon convert. Many of them wrote accounts of their spiritual journey and a number of lists of the most prestigious converts were published by W. Gordon Gorman in the 1880s, 1890s and 1900s under the title *Converts to Rome* (see p. 63); some were alphabetical but others were divided by category.

There must be thousands of written accounts by converts of their reasons for becoming Catholics, but, as with testimonies given by converts to other forms of Christianity, there is no systematic way of finding them.

Catholic schools and orphanages

The records of 19th century Catholic schools are just like those for Anglican schools. Some were private and fee-paying; others were for poor children and funded by charity. They were usually central to the concerns of the parish and figure largely in its history. Funding was available from the state on terms that were not always acceptable, and there were various political battles. The day-to-day records of the school may or may not have survived, but its activities are bound to have been reported in the newspapers from time to time. Catholic teachers were trained at a small number of training colleges – the most important were Notre Dame in Liverpool for women and Brook Green, Hammersmith, in London for men.

The PRO has records of the applications of many Catholic schools for funding and also has the reports of HM Inspectors. These go into a great deal of detail about the school and the teachers but are not likely to single out individual children.

Where they survive, school admission books usually indicate previous school attended and this can be vital in tracing the movement of families.

From the 1860s most dioceses established a range of specifically Catholic institutions for the needy, mostly run by religious orders. The most usual were orphanages, industrial schools and homes for the elderly, but there were also special schools for the blind and the deaf and various other groups. Details of these are given each year in the *Catholic Directory*. Many survive and have their own records; where the institution has closed, the records are probably with the archivist of the religious order concerned; if not, they may be with the diocesan archivist or, less likely, in the local record office.

Residential care, fostering, adoption and child migration

The modern Catholic caring services run by the various dioceses and religious orders continue to provide help and support for people in need. They are well aware that, for some people, tracing their background is more than a hobby. For those in residential care, who were adopted or fostered, or who emigrated, a comprehensive service is available. In many cases, however, the older files contain only facts (date of admission, name of person making the admission, physical details of the child) rather than the personal history and motives that people are hoping for. This is especially true when the child was transferred to a Catholic institution from the local authority, rather than from the courts or other organizations.

One warning in this sensitive area. People often remember having been told that there were no records, but it may be that they asked the wrong person. Employees often think there are no old records because they have never seen them, whereas in fact the records were transferred to an archive or central repository many years ago and are both safe and available.

Full addresses of the diocesan care societies can be found in the *Catholic Directory*. For enquiries about possible records of children in care, write to the Catholic Child Welfare Council, who if possible will send your letter on to the appropriate organization.

▼ Catholic Child Welfare Council
St Joseph's Centre
Watford Way
Hendon
London NW4 4TY
Email: ccwc@compuserve.com

Records of priests and nuns

In the 19th and 20th centuries most English and Welsh parish priests have trained to work in their home diocese – they were known as seculars and were answerable to their bishop. Their careers are easy to follow, initially through the *Catholic Directory*. A great deal can be found about their lives from standard sources and personal memories (as they were obviously very conspicuous in the parishes where they worked). In a number of dioceses short biographies of every priest have been published.

Some men chose to join a religious order. Their careers are usually well documented by their order and the archivist is usually happy to give family members details of their relative's life. The main orders working in this country are the Benedictines, Dominicans, Franciscans and Jesuits. There are also other orders that are smaller nationally, but still very significant in the areas where they work.

The careers of nuns are equally well documented. More than 90 congregations existed in England and Wales by 1900 and it is estimated that over 20,000 women had entered Catholic religious orders in this country by 1914. Most of the orders were active, running schools, orphanages, hospitals and old people's homes; others led highly energetic lives on the foreign missions. Many of these women too were Irish, Belgian, French or German, as well as English. Many were committed converts, often with surprising family connections amongst Anglicans and nonconformists.

Many people do not know which order their relative belonged to. The *Catholic Directory* lists those who were parish priests, but all men working in England and Wales are listed in C. Fitzgerald-Lombard, *English and Welsh Priests 1801–1914* (see p. 63). There is no central index of nuns, but CFS and CAS have cooperated to produce a database of nuns who entered their order before 1914, and this so far covers about 60 orders and 14,000 women.

The records of most of the religious orders are excellent and, if approached tactfully, most archivists are very pleased to see their records used and their deceased sisters celebrated.

Directories and newspapers

The first Catholic almanac was the *Laity's Directory* (1768–1839), the main purpose of which was to record where and when Mass could be found. It steadily expanded to include advertisements, religious notices and appeals. There was also a substantial section of obituaries and these were reprinted in CRS vol. 12 (see p. 15).

The *Laity's Directory* was followed by the *Catholic Directory* (1838+), which continues to appear every year.

Catholic newspapers developed in the early 19th century, but many of them were short-lived and concentrated on the fight for Irish Catholic emancipation. In the later 19th century a number of papers were founded, most of which still survive. The most important are:

The Dublin Review (1836+)
The Tablet (1840+)
The Rambler (1846–61)
The Universe (1860+)
The Month (1864+)
The Catholic Fireside (1879–1978)
The Catholic Herald (1888+)

The *Catholic Herald* developed a large number of local editions and there was an increasing number of local

Catholic newspapers, as well as diocesan ones. Many larger parishes published a parish magazine, as did most of the children's societies, missionary organizations and Catholic societies such as the SVP and the Catenians. Many other Catholic periodicals are primarily about religion, but almost all contain articles about people and places, whether local or connected with good causes for which they were trying to raise money.

Obviously Catholics may appear in any other newspapers or periodicals in connection with matters where their religion is irrelevant. Local Catholic news, particularly school news, is likely to be reported in the local newspapers as being of general interest.

In football and other sports, many teams were based on a parish youth club and may be reported in the sports news with photographs of the team.

Non-Catholic records of Catholics: pointers on basic sources

General registration

In theory all births, marriages and deaths have been registered in England and Wales from July 1837. Neither the indexes nor the certificates take any account of religion; nor did Catholics have any objection to registration.

The national indexes are held at the Family Records Centre, but are increasingly available in local record offices or local studies libraries, or through family history societies. For more information, see the PRO Pocket Guide *Using Birth, Marriage and Death Records*.

There are a number of reasons why you may have difficulty finding entries on Catholic ancestors:

- Registration of births was not compulsory in the early years and, apart from indifference, many new arrivals from Ireland may not have realized there was such a system. However, Catholics are almost certain to have had a baby baptized, so there should be evidence of the birth date in church records.

- Registrars are often unfamiliar with Irish names and this may mean that the entry is not where the researcher expects to find it in the index. In particular, the use of 'O' in front of many Irish names was not as common in the mid-19th century as it became later.

- When the whole family was ill, even deaths may not have been registered. This was not the doctor's responsibility, and neither undertakers nor gravediggers were likely to leave a diseased body unburied just because paperwork was missing. Evidence of death should be available either from church burial registers or cemetery records.

There is a chance that entries missing in the central indexes can be found in the records of the local registrar of births, marriages and deaths.

Census

The 1901 census will be available online from 2 January 2002, with access at libraries, record offices and the FRC as well as at home. Microfiche will be available at the PRO and many libraries and record offices; however it will not offer the index and search benefits of the internet version. Microfilms of the censuses from 1841–91, taken at 10-year intervals, are held at the FRC. However, most local record offices and local studies libraries hold copies for their area.

Catholics appear without distinction in all the censuses from 1841. The problem of finding those who were not living in family groups (servants, schoolchildren, those on holiday or in lodging houses) are often solved by indexes. However, the enumerators' attempts to spell Irish surnames may mean entries are difficult to recognize (e.g. 'Defi' for 'Duffy'). If in doubt, check against the original. For more information, see the PRO Pocket Guide *Using Census Returns*.

Wills

Wills from 1858 are held at the Principal Registry of the Family Division, but the indexes are available on microfiche at many locations, including the FRC and the SoG.

▼ **Principal Registry of the Family Division**
First Avenue House
42–9 High Holborn
London WC1V 6NP
Telephone: 020 7947 6000

Catholic wills were proved with those of everyone else in local bishops' courts until 1857, and in the state system thereafter. Their religion may be shown by the legacies they leave or instructions about their funeral. All nuns were supposed to make a will, and these should have been proved in the usual way. Many Catholics had relatives and property out of England, so their wills may give vital clues as to their origins. For more information, see the PRO Pocket Guide *Using Wills*.

Gravestones

Until the establishment of private cemeteries in the late 1830s and borough cemeteries in 1853, almost all Catholics were buried in the local Anglican churchyard and might have a gravestone there. They were cautious about drawing attention to their religion, however, and the wording is usually indistinguishable from that on Anglican gravestones. By the late 19th century Catholic phraseology (such as 'RIP' and 'Of your charity pray for the soul of') was very popular with high Anglicans.

Most borough cemeteries established a Catholic section sooner or later, and in the meantime the name of the minister or priest who took the service can easily be checked to see if he was Catholic. Most Catholics, like most Anglicans, were buried in public graves and could not afford a marker.

In some country areas the new Catholic churches had their own cemetery, but in urban areas this was rarely possible, except in a few large towns. In Liverpool the Catholic cemeteries have computerized their records, and a similar project is ongoing at Moston in Manchester. In London the early records of the two Catholic cemeteries (Kensal Green and Leytonstone) have been transcribed and indexed by the CFHS. Copies are available in the CCL and SoG.

Practising Catholics have not really adopted cremation, but people change religion and some of your relatives may not be buried where you expect.

Records of property and work

Catholics appear without distinction in records of property, including deeds and conveyances, rate books, poll books and electors' lists. They appear in company registrations and bankruptcy records; they also appear in commercial directories and advertise their businesses.

Working-class Catholics were members of trade unions and friendly societies. However, at local level there may have been either anti-Catholic or anti-Irish prejudice (often both). The Irish were often amongst the blacklegs brought in by employers to break a strike, and this could lead to a legacy of bitterness. Orange Lodges were very active in Lancashire and sectarian rivalry between different groups of Irish was widespread. Some firms were known to favour Catholics, so this prejudice could work in their favour as well as against them.

Throughout the 19th century about 40 per cent of soldiers in the British Army were of Irish origin; many of these were

Catholic, although religion is not shown in the early records. There were very few Catholic officers until the First World War. The same applies to a lesser extent in the Royal Navy. From the 18th century local priests were paid an allowance for work with Catholics stationed locally and this was very important in towns such as Portsmouth, Chelsea and Chatham. Full-time chaplains were employed in the army in the 1850s and in the navy in the 1860s.

The Catholic Chaplaincy in Aldershot has a small number of sacramental registers, which have all been copied and can be found at CCL and SoG. The Catholic Chaplaincy has nothing else of a historical nature and there is no need for family historians to contact it.

A great many Catholics were killed during the First and Second World Wars, and their names appear on parish and school war memorials and rolls of honour.

Lastly, at any time there were a great many Catholics in prison, both as wardens and inmates. Prisoners' registers at the PRO give religious denomination from about 1850.

The Poor Law

Most records relating to the Poor Law before 1834 are with the parish records in the local record office. From 1834 they are with the records of the Boards of Guardians, which should be in the local record office. For more information, see the PRO Pocket Guide *Using Poor Law Records*.

Poor Catholics mostly lived in towns and received poor relief on the same terms as everyone else, except that the laws of settlement (residence qualifications) were operated differently (less rigidly) in the case of Irish and Scottish people. This was a question of nationality, not religion.

Large numbers of poor Catholics spent time in work-houses, and the Catholic authorities were concerned about access to religious services, especially for children. The establishment of creed registers defined a person's religion at the time of their admission and provided some protection. These registers will be with the other workhouse records. As Catholics became able to fund their own orphanages and industrial schools, it was possible for children in public care, whether through the workhouses or the courts, to be transferred to Catholic institutions and, in the modern phrase, to take their funding with them.

Anglican church records

It might be thought that these would be irrelevant to Catholics, but it has already been noted that from 1754 to 1837 all Catholics were married in the Anglican church and until 1853 almost all Catholics were buried there.

There are less likely to be baptisms of practising Catholics and such baptisms are probably evidence of lapsation – but that itself is part of family history, and any avenue should be followed.

Schools including Anglican schools

Many children of Catholics, especially in mixed marriages, did not attend Catholic schools. They are likely to appear in Anglican or state school records without comment.

ⓘ Remember

From 1837 most families are traced through state records. Consult general registration of births, marriages and deaths, and censuses, wills, and borough cemeteries first.

Many Catholic parish records are still with the parish priest. Either he or the parish secretary will probably undertake a certain amount of searching for you, but these are not public records. Consider sending a donation with your request.

All Catholic parishes should have baptism, confirmation and marriage registers. It depends on luck whether they have anything else. Details of Catholic registers to 1880 will be found in M. Gandy, *Catholic Missions and Registers 1700–1880,* and a short history of the foundation of each parish to 1907 in B. W. Kelly, *Historical Notes on English Catholic Missions* (see p. 62).

PART TWO:
THE PENAL PERIOD 1559–1829

Suppression of Catholicism was very effective in many parts of England and Wales, but there were still quite large numbers of Catholics as late as 1600 in areas that would later be a Catholic desert. Catholic survival was greatest in the northern counties. In the west, south and east of England Catholic communities could survive only where the local gentry were Catholic themselves and could offer protection from the laws – if only because they were the local magistrates who had a duty to enforce them! Catholic gentry sometimes even had control of the appointment of Anglican vicars in their parish, and many Catholic nobles have a magnificent monument in the parish church – with no mention of their religion.

Catholic practice became illegal again when Elizabeth I became queen, and the Act of Uniformity imposed a fine of one shilling for non-attendance at church. Elizabeth was no fanatic and hoped that the old Catholics would simply die out.

Active persecution began in 1581 in response to a changed political climate, and a new Act provided for the death penalty for reconciling or being reconciled to the Catholic church. Many priests were hung, drawn and quartered over the next 20 years. Hearing Mass now attracted a fine of 100 marks, and failure to attend Anglican services carried a fine of £5 per week. People who refused to attend services were known as 'recusants'. However, there was always a very real distinction between being a 'known' or 'suspected' Catholic and being a 'convicted' Catholic, i.e., one who had been formally presented at quarter sessions (court sessions) and convicted under the Act.

In 1587 the law was stiffened and the £20 fines went on accumulating until the recusant conformed. This made an annual fine of £260, multiplied a number of times in some cases, and many recusants were unable to pay even if they wanted to. In that case, the recusant's goods and two-thirds of his lands were forfeited.

For the next few years recusants were under very great pressure, and many submitted and conformed. As for those who did not, as well as suffering from financial pressure many were imprisoned for offering protection to priests and for having Catholic services in their houses.

The deaths of Elizabeth I in 1603 and her minister Robert Cecil in 1611 changed the climate for Catholics. The Gunpowder Plot of 1605 fixed the public image of Catholics as untrustworthy, but James I and Charles I were tolerant. Their wives were Catholic, and Catholic services were held within the royal palaces. Recusants could now expect to bargain over their annual fines, and Catholics who were too poor to be fined were usually left alone.

Catholics sided with the Royalists in the Civil War (1642–6), but Cromwell was too preoccupied with the chaos of Puritan religious sects to worry about Catholics in the 1650s.

After the Restoration of Charles II (1660) Catholics suffered persecution again, but the real focus was on Protestant nonconformists, and it is often impossible to tell from the quarter sessions records whether individuals were 'papists', 'sectaries', 'anabaptists' or Quakers. Quakers themselves complained at being brought before the courts under anti-Catholic legislation. The phrase 'convicted recusant', which almost certainly means a Catholic in the pre-Civil War period, may mean any form of non-Anglican in the years 1662–85.

Anti-Catholic feeling fuelled the Titus Oates Plot of 1678, and a number of innocent Catholics were imprisoned and executed.

The situation changed for a few years under the Catholic King James II (1685–8). After his abdication Catholics were back in their previous position except that they were now assumed to be Jacobites as well. It was now illegal for a Catholic to inherit land, and Catholics were obliged to establish complicated trusts to secure their incomes for their heirs. These laws remained in force until 1778. The last Catholic priest to be sentenced to life imprisonment was John Baptist Moloney in 1767 (although in fact he served only three years).

In 1778 freedom of worship was granted to Catholics, and in 1791 they were given permission to build public chapels. A number of other anti-Catholic statutes were repealed in 1829, but this mostly affected the middle and upper classes.

Catholic numbers had declined steadily, but not dramatically, and by 1767 Catholics are estimated to have been about 1 per cent of the population, although heavily concentrated in certain pockets. From then on, numbers increased more or less in proportion with the population until the 1840s.

Catholic records of Catholics

Seminary, college and convent records

In 1568 Cardinal Allen founded an English college at Douai in northern France to ensure that there would be a trained priesthood if England became Catholic again. Over the following years many more colleges were founded in France, the Spanish Netherlands, Italy, Spain and Portugal, and large numbers of young Catholics were sent abroad to be educated, whether they were intended for the priesthood or not. From 1598 a parallel series of convents were founded, so that by 1660 there were about 40 specifically English Catholic institutions on the Continent.

These organizations became like extended families as generation after generation returned to them. They had a deep sense of being exiles for the Faith, and in the late 16th and 17th centuries they were aware that the young men they sent back to England were very likely to die on the scaffold. As they were all in safe Catholic countries, they kept extensive records and much of what we know about undercover Catholicism was written by them.

Most of these institutions returned to England in 1793 and a number still survive. Many of their archivists are members of CAS, and a great many of their records have been published by CRS. M. Gandy, *Catholic Family History: a Bibliography of General Sources* (see p. 64) gives other printed sources.

Priests and martyrs

All priests were in hiding until the 18th century, and a great deal is still unknown about them. The lives of those who were martyred (about 180 in all) were often written at the time, and their family background noted if they were Catholic or prominent. Many of the more ordinary priests of Protestant background have not yet been researched by family historians.

Almost all priests took a false name, but this was usually a name that would be recognizable to those who knew them and it often provides an important genealogical clue.

D. A. Bellenger, *English and Welsh Priests 1558–1800* and C. Fitzgerald-Lombard, *English and Welsh Priests 1801–1914* (see p. 63) provide the simplest summary of all priests who were trained for England and Wales. There are good biographical dictionaries of secular priests and those in many of the religious orders (see p. 62–4).

M. Hodgetts, *Secret Hiding Places* (see p. 64) is an authoritative account of this romantic aspect of the days of 'rack and rope'.

Catholic mission registers

These have already been described on p. 22. Where they exist, they are very important – but only half a dozen small registers are known from before 1700 and most do not begin until the 1740s or later.

Bishops' confirmation registers

There was no Catholic bishop in England from 1632 until 1687, when Bishop Leyburn was appointed. He immediately set out on a tour of northern England, and the names of 20,000 people (12,000 in Lancashire) whom he confirmed have been published by the North West Catholic History Society. After the abdication of James II, England and Wales were divided into four districts administered by Vicars Apostolic. Those for the Midlands District (which covered 15 counties) recorded confirmations centrally in the years 1768 to 1815, and those for the London District (which covered the Home Counties and the Channel Islands) did so in the years 1826 to 44. Both volumes have been published by the CFHS.

Estate and family papers

Catholicism in the 17th and 18th centuries was very much an upper-class religion. Priests could not work without safe houses as their base, and only in parts of Lancashire and the North Yorkshire moors did yeoman communities manage without the gentry's protection. The Catholic gentry, which suffered greatly (both in financial and career terms), were very committed to their religion and it usually plays a very important part in their papers.

The Royal Commission on Historical Manuscripts exists to centralize information on the whereabouts of personal and estate papers, and their computer database is accessible online. For their address, see p. 20.

Non-Catholic records of Catholics

The most important records of Catholics in the 16th to 18th centuries are those of the quarter sessions, at which Catholics were regularly reported for not attending church. Recusant rolls record the fines imposed on richer Catholics. In the 18th century registration of papists' estates gives us the names of both gentry and tenants. There are a number of national lists of Catholics (1705, 1767, 1780) in the Parliamentary Archives (see p. 19), but the local material from which these were drawn up will usually also be found in local quarter sessions records.

At county level many Catholics families were socially important, and their pedigrees are readily available in the standard sources for the gentry.

From the early 17th century poor Catholics were usually left alone, and we therefore have very little information about how many there were in the towns. The most Catholic counties were Lancashire, Northumberland,

Durham, Staffordshire, Worcestershire and the North Riding of Yorkshire. London had a great many Catholics, but not as a percentage of its population. Many were visitors based elsewhere.

The following are the most important records.

Anglican records
(Usually in the local record office;
sometimes in separate diocesan archives)

In practice the marriages and burials of most of the gentry and a high proportion of the yeomanry will still be found in the Anglican parish registers; where there are gaps they are usually in the baptisms. Catholics took out marriage licences, proved their wills and put up memorial inscriptions, just as their neighbours did.

Catholics may appear in the ecclesiastical courts but were more likely to be cited at quarter sessions, because non-attendance at church was against the law. It was punished by fines rather than excommunication. However, most Bishops' Visitations asked whether there were any Catholics or nonconformists in the parish, and vicars often listed them. There are a great many such lists in Anglican diocesan archives in the late 17th and early 18th centuries.

Quarter sessions
(Local record office; often in print)

The records of quarter sessions are the most important source for the names of ordinary Catholics. In some areas long lists were presented regularly and the same names appear time after time for years. Probably no lists are complete, and it is impossible to tell why names appear some years and not others.

The records may give a false impression: usually we cannot tell (a) whether people cited were actually present and (b) whether fines imposed were actually collected.

The government frequently wanted to know how many Catholics there were, and quarter sessions were then asked to produce lists.

Exchequer pipe rolls
(PRO, E 372)

The fines imposed by the 1581 Act were payable to the crown. They were paid into the exchequer and from 1581 to 1592 the names of those fined (about 2,500 people) appear in the pipe rolls. Fortunately they have all been extracted and published in CRS vol. 71 (see p. 15). The names are arranged alphabetically, so repetitions are easy to identify.

Recusant rolls
(PRO, E 376 and E 377 (duplicate series))

By 1592 the number of forfeitures enrolled in the pipe rolls had become so great that a separate series of recusant rolls was established. It runs from 1592 to 1691 with some breaks. The rolls are arranged by county and include the lands or goods seized, the name of the recusant, the rent due to the crown, the name of the crown's lessee, if any, arrears of payment and notes of payments made, the total debt and other details. As often in recusancy (and other) proceedings, the authority to proceed is not evidence that anyone did proceed. Separate research is needed to show whether the lands that were technically forfeited were actually seized.

It is always worth looking at the names of those who leased forfeited lands from the crown. They were quite likely to be friends or relatives of the convicted recusants, ensuring that the lands did not go out of the family.

The first four rolls (1592–6) have been published in CRS vols 18, 57 and 61 (see p. 15). The introduction to vol. 57 explains in detail how the system worked. The Middlesex rolls for the reign of James I were abstracted by J. J. LaRocca and published in CRS vol. 76. As everyone who appears in this material was of reasonable financial standing, the remaining rolls are probably the most important untapped source for 17th-century gentry Catholicism. However, they are not easy to use.

The strict operation of the laws in the 1580s had given way by the 1620s to a much more flexible approach. The Northern Book of Compositions (1629–32), published in CRS vol. 53, gives an insight into the sort of compromises that were reached. The figures agreed were certainly returned to the exchequer.

The crime of recusancy was not explicitly confined to Catholics, and from 1662 there is an unknown percentage of Protestant dissenters in the recusant rolls.

Registration of papists' and nonjurors' estates
(PRO, E 174)

After the Jacobite Rebellion of 1715 all Catholics refusing to take the oaths of loyalty and supremacy were required to register their names and estates at quarter sessions (the use of the word 'estate' may give a false impression of wealth). The returns describe the property and give the names of the tenants with details of tenure and the amount of rent payable, so they are an important source for yeomen as well as gentry.

A full list of the owners' names is in the series list and summaries were published in J. O. Payne, *Records of the English Catholics of 1715* (see p. 64). The obligation remained on the statute book until 1778. The returns for Lancashire and Durham have been published by the Lancashire and Cheshire Record Society and the Surtees Society, and have been taken from the material in quarter sessions.

The returns of papists, 1705, 1767, 1780
(Parliamentary Archives; also amongst
quarter sessions records)

These three attempts to produce a national census of Catholics are held at the Parliamentary Archives. The version for 1767 is arranged in dioceses by town or village and lists people in household groups, giving age, relationship, occupation and number of years resident in the parish. It was published by CRS in two volumes in 1980 and 1990.

The 1767 return of papists is the most important source for the 18th century. Unfortunately the Parliamentary Archives returns do not give names, just initials, for most of the country. However, the originals in local quarter sessions records usually give full names. Many have been published.

The following can be useful, especially for more prosperous families.

State Papers (PRO)

The State Papers Domestic relate to every matter with which government was concerned and therefore contain a vast amount of material, sometimes systematic and sometimes random. Fortunately they are calendared (summarized) up to 1704 and there are indexes to the calendars. Start with the index references to Catholics, papists, recusants or Roman Catholics, but references to treason, trials and oaths or just to the relevant counties or important gentry may turn up useful material; the keywords are different at different periods.

The material itself is on microfilm on open access. There are a great many lists of Catholics over the years, mostly arranged by county. However, it is probable that they are all incomplete!

State Papers Foreign and the State Papers relating to various Catholic countries contain many letters and comments on the English situation, but very little material applicable to ordinary families.

Privy Council and Treasury papers (PRO)

These vast series, both well-calendared for the 17th century, contain a certain amount of random material on Catholics – for example, licences allowing named convicted recusants to travel more than 5 miles from their homes. The only approach, unless you are guided by a specific reference, is to browse imaginatively in the indexes.

Assize records (PRO)

These include Catholics tried as criminals, particularly the priests and lay people who harboured them; many were eventually executed. Note that until the 19th century people were held in prison *until* their trial, not usually after it.

The Lord Treasurer's Remembrancer's memoranda rolls
(PRO, E 368)

These records relate to the discharge of crown debtors and therefore include those Catholics who chose to conform to the Church of England and then recover sequestrated lands and be discharged of their recusancy fines. The convicted recusant could not free himself simply by paying the fines. In any case, government was more concerned with conformity than income and a conforming recusant was likely to see the outstanding fine waived, or anyway ignored. However, there was a set procedure, thorough and very well documented, for conforming. In practice a certain amount of 'conversion' was only temporary and some people appear a number of times both in the recusant rolls and the significations of conformity in this series.

The procedure itself was ecclesiastical, but had to be certified to the Exchequer Revenue Court, which discharged crown debtors. Arranged by county and name, the information given includes name, rank, dates of convictions, debts, and dates and places of conformity and receiving communion and of taking the Oaths of Allegiance and Supremacy. The names of those conforming in the years 1590 to 1625 were published in *Catholic Ancestor* between June 1995 and November 1996.

Lay subsidies (PRO, E 179)

This important series of taxes was paid by everyone, but foreigners, and Catholics paid double so are easy to recognize. (This does not apply to the hearth tax returns, which are also part of this series).

Committee for Compounding with Delinquents 1643–60 (PRO, SP 23)

The victorious Parliamentary government set out to fine all royalists, based on a percentage of the value of their lands or goods, but was willing to do a deal. Many royalists were recusants, and this is stated. This material is published in *Calendar of Proceedings of the Committee for Compounding* (HMSO, 5 vols).

There are inventories of Catholic possessions in SP 28. After the Restoration a committee was established to compound with those who had purchased sequestered estates (see PRO, E 178).

Sacrament certificates (PRO, C 224, C 214, E 195, KB 22, CHES 4)

These are certificates produced as evidence that someone had taken the Oath of Supremacy and Anglican communion. Catholics should not be in them, so appearance is evidence of either apostasy or hypocrisy.

The Commission for Superstitious Lands (PRO, SP)

In the atmosphere of anti-Catholic and anti-Jacobite suspicion in the 1690s, it was easy for plotters to harass and blackmail Catholics by formal means. A number of commissions of enquiry ordered at this time (see State Papers) were clearly dishonestly motivated, and their actions in Lancashire contributed substantially to the Lancashire Plot. The background is given in P. A. Hopkins, 'The Commission for Superstitious Lands of the 1690s' (*Recusant History* 15(4), October 1980).

Land tax
(Local record offices; some material in the PRO)

This tax was instituted in 1692 and Catholics were obliged to pay double. The PRO has a national return for 1798 in IR 23, plus some appeals by Catholics against the necessity to pay double. They considered the requirement should have been repealed when Catholicism was made legal, but in fact it remained until 1829.

There is some material relating to papists' double payments in the PRO (E 182), and some certificates showing that land formerly held by Catholics was now held by Protestants in PRO E 174/1/35–42.

Forfeited Estates Commission: FEC (PRO)

The Commission was established after the Jacobite Rising of 1715 and many Catholics, especially from Lancashire and Northumberland, were involved. The enrolment of papists' estates in quarter sessions was first copied to this commission. Some extracts were published in E. Estcourt and J. O. Payne, *English Catholic Nonjurors of 1715* (Burnes and Oates, 1888), mostly relating to Lancashire. Further extracts, also mostly relating to Lancashire, were published in J. O. Payne, *Records of the English Catholics of 1715* (see p. 64). Material relating to the trials of Jacobites will be found at the PRO in ASSI 41–7, CHES 21 and 24, DURH 17, PL 25–8 and SP 35.

Close rolls (PRO, C 54)

This is a vast source, not reasonable to browse. It includes records of land surrendered or forfeited by traitors, papists, royalists or Jacobites. Catholic wills were supposed to be enrolled there from 1717 to 1778 and the list of these, fairly short, was published in *The Genealogist* (NS no. 1 p. 267 and no. 2 pp. 59–60, 279–82). Clearly many wills were not included.

Oaths of Allegiance and Supremacy (PRO)

Certificates of recusants (and nonjurors) refusing to swear the oath prescribed under the Security of the Sovereign Act 1714 are in C 203/6.

For 200 years Catholics had refused the Oath of Supremacy. From 1778 a form of words was developed that was acceptable to them. Catholic oaths of loyalty 1778–86, 1791–1822 and 1839–57 giving names, addresses and occupations are in E 169; others are in CP 37 (1778–1829) and C 214/21 (1830, 1837–8); attorneys (1831–7) are in E 3 and solicitors in Chancery (1791–1813) in C 217/180/5.

Catholic Attorneys' admission rolls 1790–1836
(PRO, CP 10)

After Catholicism was made legal, Catholic attorneys were allowed to swear a different oath from Anglicans.

Non-parochial registers
(PRO, RG 4, but widely available on microfilm, including at the FRC)

The catalogue details the Catholic registers that have been deposited; almost all of them relate to the north-eastern counties of Northumberland, Durham and Yorkshire. Full details of their coverage are given in M. Gandy, *Catholic Missions and Registers 1700–1880* (see p. 62).

A description of what they are likely to contain appears in Part One (see pp. 23–5).

Register of places of worship (PRO, RG 31)

From 1791 Catholics were allowed to register places of worship. In 1852 the law was amended to require certification to the Registrar General and both clerks and bishops' or archdeacons' registrars were required to draw up a return of all the places of meeting that had been certified to them since the beginning. This series is therefore in principle an easy way into the more extensive and detailed records in quarter sessions and diocesan records.

There are two full series, which ought in principle to contain different material. Entries are likely to describe the house, often in terms of who owned or occupied it, and to give the parish and the names of those certifying. Certification shows intention but is not evidence that the building was ever used for religious services or, if it was, for how long.

Census of religious worship, 1851 (PRO, HO 129)

This is not as useful as it sounds. There is a one-page form for each place of worship giving figures of the numbers who attended the services. The only name likely to appear is that of the priest. The returns for many local areas have been published, and a photocopy of the Catholic returns for the whole of England and Wales is in the library of the SoG.

ⓘ Remember

From 1559 to 1778 Catholicism was illegal in this country. Some things we as family historians would like to know were not recorded. There was no formal church organization, so most of the relevant records were made by the state, the Anglican church or private individuals.

A great deal has been published, especially by the Catholic Record Society, the Catholic Family History Society, the local societies and many of the religious orders. A full analysis of what is in print (to 1996) will be found in M. Gandy, *Catholic Family History: a Bibliography of General Sources* and *Catholic Family History: a Bibliography of Local Sources* (see p. 64). However, a great deal of original research still remains to be done.

FURTHER READING

Records

J. Gibson and P. Peskett, *Record Offices: How to Find Them* (FFHS).

J. A. Williams, 'Sources for Recusant History (1559–1791) in English Official Archives', in *Recusant History* 16(4) (CRS, October 1983).

Missions and their registers

M. Gandy, *Catholic Missions and Registers 1700–1880* (6 vols including Scotland) (London: Michael Gandy, 1994).

M. Gandy, *Catholic Parishes in England, Wales and Scotland: An Atlas* (London: Michael Gandy, 1994).

B. W. Kelly, *Historical Notes on English Catholic Missions* (London: Kegan, Paul, Trench, Trübner, 1907, Michael Gandy, 1995).

There are also a number of detailed diocesan histories (e.g. Middlesbrough, Nottingham, Salford, Shrewsbury) and many hundreds of individual mission histories. Copies of many of these are in the Catholic Central Library.

Biography and family history

Catholics appear in all the standard sources, and many histories of the older missions are in practice histories of the gentry families which protected them.

M. Bence-Jones, *The Catholic Families* (London: Constable, 1992).

J. Gillow, *Bibliographical Dictionary of the English Catholics* (London: Burnes and Oates, 1887–1902, 1999).

W. Gordon-Gorman, *Converts to Rome* (London: Sands, various edns 1884–1910).

The Catholic Who's Who (London: Burns and Oates, 34th edn, 1941; 35th edn, 1952).

The clergy/religious

G. Anstruther, *The Seminary Priests* (Great Wakering, Essex: Mayhew-McCrimmon, 1800, 1969–1977).

D. A. Bellenger, *English and Welsh Priests 1558–1800* (Bath: Downside Abbey, 1984).

H. N. Birt, *Obit Book of the English Benedictines 1600–1912* (Edinburgh, 1913, 1970).

C. Fitzgerald-Lombard, *English and Welsh Priests 1801–1914* (Bath: Downside Abbey, 1993).

H. Foley, *Records of the English Province of the Society of Jesus* (London: Burns and Oates, 1877–1883).

W. Gumbley, *Obituary Notices of the English Dominicans from 1555 to 1952* (London: Blackfriars, 1955).

F. M. Steele, *The Convents of Great Britain* (London: Sands, 1902).

Fr Thaddeus, *The Franciscans in England 1600–1850* (London: Art and Book Company, 1898).

B. Zimmerman, *Carmel in England* (London: Burns and Oates, 1899).

Martyrs and prisoners

Anon, *The Martyrs of England and Wales 1535–1680* (Catholic Truth Society, 1985).

R. Challoner, *Memoirs of Missionary Priests* (London: Burns, Oates and Washbourne, 1924).

M. Hodgetts, *Secret Hiding Places* (Dublin: Veritas Publications, 1989)

Jacobites

HMSO, *The Records of the Forfeited Estates Commission* (HMSO, 1965)

J. O. Payne, *Records of the English Catholics of 1715* (London: Burns and Oates, 1889)

Other material

For an analysis of other available material in print, see four books by Michael Gandy (London: Michael Gandy, 1996):

Catholic Family History: A Bibliography of General Sources

Catholic Family History: A Bibliography of Local Sources

Catholic Family History: A Bibliography for Scotland

Catholic Family History: A Bibliography for Wales